Pigs, Nerds and Macho Men

by

Lucille Cassarino
and
Mary Jean Orlando

PublishAmerica
Baltimore

© 1999 by Lucille Cassarino and Mary Jean Orlando.

All rights reserved. No part of this book may be reproduced in any form without written permission from the publishers, except by a reviewer who may quote brief passages in a review to be printed in a newspaper or magazine.

First printing

ISBN: 1-59129-473-8
PUBLISHED BY PUBLISHAMERICA BOOK PUBLISHERS
www.publishamerica.com
Baltimore

Printed in the United States of America

Dedication

This book is dedicated to the memory of Anthony Geidel.

Acknowledgements

The authors would like to thank the following people:

Kathryn Leigh Scott for putting us on the right track; Steven Swidler for his advice; Frank Bianco for his helpful suggestions; Patricia and Michael Orlando for their support; Lawrence and Vincenza Bianco for believing in us; and special thanks to all our friends from our singles club.

Table of Contents

I. Introduction — 7

II.
1. "She's Not Hungry" — 9
2. "You Lied To Me" — 11
3. Doctor My Eyes — 13
4. "My Cookies" — 15
5. Moses/The Ten Commandments — 17
6. "What A Doll!" — 19
7. Mr. Mumbles — 23
8. Jumping Jack Flash — 25
9. "I Hear The Girls Are Pretty On The 25th Floor" — 27
10. Vincent Van Gogh — 31
11. "She Lives At Home And Her Mother Doesn't Drive" — 33
12. Mama's Boys — 37
13. The Octopus — 41
14. Pony Tail — 43
15. Nurse On Call — 47
16. "You're Going To Pay Him Rent?" — 49
17. The Dishwasher — 53
18. "You Wanna Dance?" — 55
19. The Help Me Sign — 57
20. For Whom The Bell Tolls — 59

21. The Cardinal — 61
22. The Three Little Pigs — 63
23. B.M. — 67
24. Movie Date — 69
25. Thom McCann — 71
26. "I'll Have A Bagel" — 73
27. Disco Bonnie and Sleazy Sal — 75
28. Spike — 77
29. Tod, Tad, Toad — 79
30. "Show Me The Dollar!" — 81
31. Gentleman John — 85
32. They Just Don't Get It — 89
33. Short Takes — 91
    The Chiropractor
    The Coupon Man
    Where's The Beef?
    Take Off That Head Band
    The Personal Ad
34. The Pointless Sisters — 95

III.   Epilogue — 99

Introduction

The Singles Scene, it's bizarre, and we have the stories to prove it. This book relates actual experiences that have happened to us or to our friends. Looking back, we realize that these experiences are amusing but of course they did not seem funny when they were actually happening to us.

We have also learned new vocabulary words because of the dating scene. Have you ever been told that you were G.U.? What's G.U., you ask? It's Geographically Undesirable. A lot of guys we have met do not want to travel for a date. They want you to live around the corner.

I was at a Brooklyn dance one time when a guy approached me. "Do you live in Bay Ridge?" he asked. I really did not like the looks of him, with all of that heavy gold that appeared to be permanently attached to his neck and arms, so I responded, "I live in Albany." He turned around and walked away. Guys just do not want to cross any bridges or pay any tolls!

Now a little about ourselves:

Mary Jean is a registered nurse. She went back to college, Mount Saint Vincent, to continue her education while she was working. Not an easy task. She often had to turn down an invitation to go dancing or to go to a movie because her homework came first. "I can't, I'm bogged down," she would say. Mary Jean is now teaching nursing at a vocational high school and loves it.

Lucille works for a large insurance company in New York City. She was an elementary school teacher when she first graduated from Hunter College. She is now involved in product development and regulatory compliance.

Well dear reader, we invite you to peruse the stories that follow. Maybe you can relate to some of them. We ask you, "Has this happened to you?"

"She's Not Hungry"

I saved my appetite all day in anticipation of my "dinner date" with Peter, a friendly acquaintance whose square face was framed by his dark hair and moustache. Peter, who worked as an electrician, did not exactly generate any "sparks" for me when he came to pick me up wearing a dirty cap. He was dressed shabbily in casual work clothes. As he opened his car door with his dirty fingers, a musty odor was evident from the messy interior.

When we arrived at the "upscale" restaurant he was taking me to, it turned out to be McDonald's. Well, I thought, maybe he is on a limited budget. At least I could get something good to eat, as I was famished at that point. The aroma of burgers and fries permeated the restaurant and the bright atmosphere was inviting.

As we approached the counter, the salesperson asked, "What would you like today?" Peter replied, "Oh, she's not hungry," after which he turned to me and said, "You're not hungry, right? We'll just have coffee!" I could not speak! I felt as if someone had just tied my vocal cords together. Unfortunately my stomach was still growling. Two coffees it was at $.75 each!

We sat down to enjoy the delicious "meal." Peter chose a small table against the wall near the window.

He began to tell me the story of his life. He had a history of health problems including open heart surgery; alas, his attraction to me, a nurse.

Peter lamented that his coronary bypass had taken place a number of years earlier and that generally this procedure only lasts ten years, so it was about time for another heart attack. I asked, "Are you planning on having it right now?"

"Oh," he replied, "it can happen anytime." I then advised him that the caffeine in coffee is not the best thing for his heart. He went on to describe his life living with his 84-year-old mother, her ailments and other sorrowful tales.

All the while, people were passing by with their trays adorned with hamburgers, french fries, apple pie, chicken, etc. The scent alone was enough to slay me, I was so hungry.

About two hours had passed at that point. I resembled a stray dog begging for scraps, but to no avail. I began to nibble on the Styrofoam cup. There were no refills. Only another cup for another $.75, which did not figure into Peter's budget. When Peter began to detail the anatomy of the heart, I knew I had had enough. After he described the aorta, I decided it was time to go home – and EAT! I suggested to Peter that we leave. Three and a half hours had passed at that point.

On the way home, Peter carefully retraced the directions to my house for what he thought would be the next time we went out. When we arrived at my house, I quickly slipped out of the car.

We did not go out again but I did see Peter at a community meeting a few months later. He offered to get me a cup of coffee. Probably because this one was FREE!

"You Lied To Me"

My friends and I drove out to a singles dance on Long Island. When we entered the dimly lit dance room, they went to sit at a table before all of the tables were taken. There were never enough tables and chairs for the 100-150 people who attended these dances. There were times when the room was so crowded it was difficult to move around.

I walked over to the bar area and got in line to get a soda. The fellow standing in front of me, nice-looking, blond hair neatly trimmed, dressed in a suit and tie, started mumbling to himself, "The girls here don't know how to do the cha-cha or the rumba," he said as he looked at me.

"Oh, my girlfriends and I can do those dances," I said.

"You can?" he replied. "Would you dance with me later?"

I said that I would.

I no sooner got to the table where my friends were sitting, when I felt a POUNDING on my back. I turned and saw that same fellow standing behind me. He asked me if I knew how to dance to "swing" music.

"Yes, I do. I'll dance with you," I answered.

We got on the dance floor and he was terrible. He pushed and pulled me all over, stepped on my feet, while I tried to follow him. All the while he never smiled nor spoke. He appeared to be concentrating on his dance steps, while I was hoping that he would not dislocate my shoulder.

Suddenly, he looked into my eyes and seriously said, "You lied to me."

"Excuse me?" I responded.

"You lied to me," he repeated. "You told me you could dance!"

I was so shocked I hardly knew how to respond. When I recovered from his words, I told him that men have different dance styles and that I was trying to follow his.

"OH NO!" he bellowed, "Any woman can follow me."

Mercifully the song ended and I thanked him for the dance. (I actually thanked him.)

About fifteen minutes later, I saw my friend Annie doing the cha-cha with this guy. (I had not had a chance to tell her what had happened.) While they were dancing, I later discovered, he was complaining to her about a girl who said she could dance but really could not. Of course he was referring to me but she did not know that.

"Oh, my girlfriend is a very good dancer; she'll dance with you," Annie told him.

"Oh, where is she?" he asked. Annie glanced around the room, spotted me and pointed at me. His eyes popped out of his head. Here he was complaining about me and she was sending him right back to me!

Doctor My Eyes

Linus and I knew each other through our singles club. He would greet me at the dances and we always had interesting conversations, he being a doctor and I a nurse. Linus' round face, framed by a receding hairline and wire-rimmed glasses, often conveyed a startled expression. He sometimes wore a poorly styled toupee which sat on top of his head like a rug.

After several months, Linus asked me out. However, every time the day came for us to go out, I would get a phone call 10 minutes before our date. Linus would say, "I have a fever; do you mind if we cancel?"

I would ask, "Is it yellow fever?"

Finally the day came when we actually made it out the door. Our destination was a restaurant for a relaxing dinner. We arrived at Pastina's, a nice little place near my home. I chose it because the busy dining room had a cozy appeal. Upon being seated we reviewed the menu and made our dinner choices. Linus and I exchanged small talk as he gazed fondly into my eyes.

As we were waiting for our salad to be served, I noticed all of the patrons were staring up at the ceiling. (The chandelier was nice but nothing extraordinary.) I could not figure out what the attraction was. Then I realized they were following Linus' cue. I looked across the table and

Linus was looking up displaying only the whites of his eyes. My first thought was, *Is he having a seizure?* I said, "Linus, are you alright?"

"No", he said, "I'm having a severe anxiety attack." Now I knew he liked me but I did not think I had such a dramatic effect on him! He proceeded to pull a bottle of medication out of his pocket. I identified it as an anti-anxiety agent. He took a pill and I waited for him to regain his composure. I informed the waiter that my friend was ill and that we had to leave. The waiter looked rather puzzled but he accepted our departure.

Linus insisted on driving. We traveled the short distance back to my home and Linus rested on the sofa. I gave him some tea. We talked for a while after which he was feeling much better. He then left to go home. I called him later that evening to make sure he arrived home safely.

I still see Linus at our club occasionally and hear from him at times but we never attempted to go out again.

"My Cookies!"

Our girlfriend Billie is petite, with long brown hair and brown eyes. When we first met her, she worked for a computer company developing educational training programs for personal computers.

It was early June when one of Billie's clients, a cookie company, was sending about 15 of its Virginia employees to New York for a week of training classes which Billie was teaching. Billie was all excited about finally meeting these people with whom she had been communicating through e-mail.

The training week came and went and we heard all about it as she drove us to a Saturday night dance. Since the people were from another state, they all wanted to see New York City while they were staying here. Several evenings after work, Billie and some of her co-workers volunteered as tour guides for the out-of-towners. As Billie told us about visiting the Statue of Liberty, the Empire State Building and seeing a Broadway play, we noticed that she kept talking a lot about Dan. Billie finally admitted that she was smitten with Dan and had the impression that he was interested in her too. When she showed us a picture of the group, we saw that Dan was chubby, a few inches taller than she, and had a smirk on his face. The day that they all left to go back to Virginia, Dan had promised that he would mail Billie a box of cookies when he got home.

The e-mail flirtation between Billie and Dan lasted all summer. They would send messages to each other at work. Dan even called her at home several times, always giving her the details of the progression of those cookies: "I'm getting the cookies. – The cookies are in my house. – The cookies are on my living room floor. – The cookies are wrapped; I just have to bring them to the post office to be mailed to you." While Billie waited for those cookies, we began to wonder if he were shipping them from China!

Then one late August evening when Billie was coming home from work, she was walking down her block towards her house, when she saw a huge truck going down her street. Now you have to know that Billie lived on a very narrow one-way street. Commercial vehicles never drove down her street; it was just too narrow. Well, sure enough, on the side of the truck in big, bold letters was the name of the cookie company where Dan worked. Was the truck delivering Billie's cookies? The truck continued slowly down her street as it passed her house. Billie could not believe it when the truck did not stop. She started chasing the truck down the block, yelling, "My cookies! My cookies!" The truck kept on going until it was out of sight. Poor Billie stopped running and stood there totally dejected, with her head down and her heart broken.

Shortly thereafter, Billie stopped hearing from Dan and to this day she still has not received those cookies!

Moses/The Ten Commandments

Mike and I seemed to have a lot in common. He was family oriented, polite and had an impressive background in science and technology. Mike was very attentive to his health and diet. He liked to cook for himself and frequented an exercise spa, which accounted for his solid, muscular build.

He came to pick me up in his sports car. We were going to a Chinese restaurant where, Mike informed me, we could enjoy an interesting, nutritious meal.

Soon after we arrived at China Palace, Mike and I were immersed in a verbal exchange of getting to know each other. As I observed Mike sitting opposite me at a small table for two, his serious manner and stern expression were evident. Mike's black side-swept hair and bushy eyebrows seemed intimidating and severe.

Suddenly Mike said, "I'd like to ask you a question if you don't mind."

"Sure," I said. I was curious, as he seemed to be in deep thought.

Mike inquired, "Have you ever broken any of the Ten Commandments?"

I heard the question but I was rather surprised to say the least. This did not seem like typical dinner conversation. "What do you mean? Which one are you alluding to?" I asked.

"Any of them," Mike replied in an authoritarian tone. "I really need a woman who has broken at least some of the commandments or she would be just too nice for me," he revealed.

"Well, I disagreed with Daddy tonight, does that count?" I asked in a lively voice.

No response from Mike.

We finished our dinner and he took me home. I began to wonder if I had dined with Moses.

Mike did not call me but later that month he showed up at a dance. He was rather quiet and subdued, not mingling too much with anyone. We exchanged greetings and spoke for a few minutes.

In keeping with "the commandments" theme, we encountered a new face, Al, that evening, strolling through the ballroom with his Bible under his arm. He seemed to be surveying the "faith community."

Al approached my friend Lolli and asked her to dance. He seemed harmless so she agreed. He put the Bible down and they walked to the dance floor. As they boogied, the new age crystal pendant hanging from Al's neck was bobbing to and fro. Al told Lolli all about his life, his three ex-wives, four grown children and his conversion to Christianity. Then he asked, "Who do you admire most in history?" My friend looked bewildered. "Don't you admire Moses?" Al asked.

Lolli exclaimed, "Moses? He's right over there!" directing Al to the table where Mike was seated. Then it was Al's turn to look bewildered!

"What A Doll!"

I usually take my glasses off at the dances. There are two reasons why I do it. One, as I am reminded by my male friends, "Men don't make passes at girls who wear glasses." Two, and most important, if I would get a good look at the guys who are at these dances, I would turn around and go home! (Sometimes it is difficult to identify the species.)

Mary Jean, Joan and I arrived at the Long Island dance. After a quick stop at the ladies room to freshen our makeup, we entered the crowded dance room. Some of our friends came over and greeted us. As I chatted with them, I removed my glasses, unaware that Henry was watching me.

After dancing with some friends, I happened to be standing by myself when a moon-faced fellow with receding hair and black-framed glasses approached me. He introduced himself as Henry and asked the usual questions: Where did I live? What did I do for a living? He said that he lived in Long Island but did not seem to mind that I resided "across the bridge." (I guess I was not G.U.) He told me about himself including that he was a child psychologist. He said that he liked it that we had similar ethnic backgrounds and that we were both professionals.

After awhile, he told me, "Put your glasses on!"

"What?" I said.

He repeated his command and added, "I like you better with them on!" I declined his directive. Then he asked how often I went to the dances. "Oh, we won't be coming to these dances anymore!" he informed me. I remained silent.

We danced a bit, then talked some more, as friends of mine came over, joined our conversation and then left us.

Henry was interesting to talk with. Throughout our conversation, he was persistent in asking for my phone number. Although I was reluctant to give it to him because I perceived him to be a controlling type of person, I finally did. Then he told me that he had to leave because he had to get up early the next morning. He said he did not want to leave before the dance ended because if he did, I might meet another guy. I told him if he had an early appointment he should leave. My friends and I were going to be leaving soon too. Then he said goodnight, told me he would call me and walked out into the hall.

About two minutes later, Mary Jean came rushing into the dance room looking like she was on a mission. She located me and came right over. "That guy Henry," she said, "he's out in the hall raving about you and screaming at the top of his lungs, "WHAT A DOLL!"

What a dope, I thought, and I gave him my phone number?

We stayed at the dance about half an hour longer. Then we said our goodbyes and went to the parking lot. Who do we see but Henry roaming around like a lost soul. "I forgot where I parked my car," he announced. We tried to be helpful but we finally had to leave him to continue his search alone.

As Joan drove us home, I told her and Mary Jean about some of the things Henry had said and about his unusual behavior. The more I thought about it, the more uncomfortable I became. I decided that if he called me I would not accept a date with him.

Two days later he called. I should have known that he would. It's the guys you want to hear from who never call. Well, Henry started talking but before he got very far, I told him that I realized it was a mistake to have given him my phone number. I said, "I'm sorry Henry, but you make me nervous."

He actually was very gracious. He said he was sorry that I was not comfortable with him. We wished each other well and hung up.

I saw him once or twice after that at a dance but we never spoke to each other again.

Mr. Mumbles

"What did you say?" That's what I said, too many times, to Rodney. It was real guesswork trying to figure out what he was saying. I thought, *maybe if I learn Morse Code I can get an edge on trying to decipher what Rodney is attempting to tell me.* I would respond with things like, "Oh that's interesting," "Sounds like fun," "That's too bad," hoping the sentiments came close to being appropriate for the conversation at hand.

Rodney, lanky with a rather disheveled appearance, always looked like he needed grooming. He wore glasses that dominated his shallow face. He always seemed to be swooping down like a big bird. He would come so close when talking or dancing with me that a paper clip could not separate us.

I always wondered if Rodney had food or marbles in his mouth, or if he was just a natural mumbler. I would never have to worry about anyone eavesdropping – they would never get a crumb of information.

Rodney mumbled equally well on the phone and in person. If there was music in the background like at a dance, it was an exceptional challenge.

Rodney always seemed oblivious to my quest for clear speech. He just kept talking and patiently repeated himself to no avail. He talked about lots of things but I never understood any of it. At the height of my frustration, I considered referring Rodney for a course in phonetics.

I think it is safe to say that Rodney's message is just "a mumble."

This was an interesting case of he said – she said, except you would never know what he said!

Jumping Jack Flash

It was a clear fall Saturday night as I rode with my friends to a dance in Upper Westchester county. Upon arriving, we greeted many other friends and acquaintances, one of whom was Jack.

Often nervous and jumpy, Jack circled around the large room, displaying an unbalanced gait. He was prematurely gray at his temples. His rugged face, defined by his bushy eyebrows and bristly moustache, faded into a corner of the room.

Colorful balloons and streamers hung above us as we enjoyed a hot buffet dinner followed by dancing. As the evening moved along, there was a raffle, dance contest and news about future club events.

Shortly after midnight, Jack announced that he was leaving. As he lived near me in the Bronx, I asked if I could ride home with him in his car since my friends were planning to remain until much later. "Sure," he said. After saying goodnight to everyone, we headed out to his car. Darkness had overtaken the evening sky.

We started out along the Taconic Parkway, heading south on a winding road with virtually no lights to illuminate our path. Jack and I were conversing as he drove. Suddenly, about 10 minutes into our trip, I noticed Jack literally jumping up out of the driver's seat and back down again.

This "reflex action" was of about 2 seconds duration. After 5 minutes it happened again, and then again, in spite of his seat belt being on.

We rode down to the Bronx with Jack jumping up and down continuously. If he had had a sun roof, he would have been driving with his head outdoors. Needless to say, I was concerned. Was he having some form of seizure or neurological syndrome? I was afraid to ask, so I did not. Jack was oblivious; he did not seem bothered by his excessive movement.

We arrived safely at my home and I thanked Jack for the (bouncy) ride. As I got out of his stunning silver Thunderbird, I watched jumping Jack ride away into the night, never to travel with him again!

"I Hear The Girls Are Pretty On The 25th Floor"

    One afternoon after lunch, I walked into the lobby of the building where I work and I noticed a fellow standing there who looked familiar. Then I realized that he was the Joe Namath lookalike that one of my girlfriends had introduced me to at a dance about a year before. He looked at me and seemed to recognize me too.
    "Aren't you Joe?" I asked. "Jenny introduced us at a Long Island dance." Joe replied that he did remember me but had forgotten my name. I told him and asked what he was doing in my building, as I remembered that he did not work for my employer. Joe was a computer programmer. He told me that he had been hired as a consultant to work on a special project that was supposed to take about six months to complete. We spoke briefly and then said goodbye.
    About a week later, my friends and I went to a Long Island dance. When we arrived, I saw Joe talking with our friend Terry. She called me over and asked if I knew Joe. I told her that I did and explained that he was working in my building. The three of us chatted for awhile. Then a friend of Terry's asked her to dance and Joe asked me. After awhile, we stopped dancing and were talking with people we knew.
    At the end of the evening, Joe, Terry and I were once

again talking together. All of a sudden, out of the blue, an animated Joe said to me, "I'd like to take you out to lunch. Do you like Chinese food?" I said that I did and that I would go to lunch with him. He asked me for my phone extension. I told him and asked if I should write it down. "No, I'll remember it," he said. Then he said that he would call me the following week.

Well, one week went by, then two, then three. As it happened, during the fourth week I ran into him by chance in the lobby. I greeted him and he was apologetic, "Oh, I forgot your number. Write it down for me and I'll call you next week." So I did.

Guess what? Again several weeks went by and no phone call. In the meantime, I had seen Terry several times at various dances. She kept asking me if Joe had taken me for that lunch date. Then one Friday evening there was a dance in Manhattan. Terry and some of my friends were meeting me for dinner before the dance. Terry told me she would meet me in the lobby of my building. Coincidentally, just as Terry arrived, Joe got off the elevator to leave for the day. Joe greeted Terry and me. He again apologized for not calling and said he would definitely call the following week. I do not know if he was embarrassed because Terry knew about the lunch date or if Terry had seen him at a dance and had said something to him but he did call me that next week.

Joe and I met at noon in the lobby and walked several blocks to a tiny neighborhood Chinese restaurant that Joe liked. The entire time he was with me he talked about other women.

He told me all about the girls he had met at the dances and what was wrong with them. This one was divorced, that one had a child, another one was interested in how much money he made, etc. After awhile I began to wonder why he asked me out in the first place.

Joe worked on the 27th floor and I was on the 22nd. While we were eating lunch Joe said, "I hear the girls are pretty on the 25th floor." I was stunned! What did he expect me to say to that?

Finally I responded, "Well, I don't know about the girls but I'll take a trip up there to check out the guys." The bill came, I offered to split it with him but he insisted on paying.

When we got back to our building, I thanked Joe for lunch and told him that we really did not have to go out for lunch since we had a cafeteria in the basement of the building that provided free lunch. (By the way, the free lunch is no longer available.)

Joe got all excited. "Oh, really?" he said. Then he promised we would have lunch once a week in the cafeteria and said he would call me the following week. As you can guess, it is quite a few years later and I still have not gotten that phone call.

Time went by and I did not run into Joe again at work nor at a dance. I assumed that his special computer project was completed and that he no longer worked for my employer.

Then about six months after that infamous lunch date, I saw Joe at a Manhattan dance. (No, Terry was not at this one.) I asked him how he was; I genuinely hoped that he had found another consulting job. Joe told me that he had and proceeded to tell me all about his new job. We talked for about half an hour when suddenly Joe announced, "Well I think I'll go over there and ask that pretty girl to dance!" I stood there with my mouth hanging open. There are so many ways to graciously take your leave of someone. There is no need to be rude! Joe could have just said, "Well it's been nice talking with you but I see some friends over there and I want to talk with them." He could have even said that he had to go to the men's room. Well, I told him that it had been nice talking with him and wished him a pleasant evening.

From then on, whenever I saw Joe at a dance I merely waved and said, "Hi," and kept on walking. I was not ever going to give him the opportunity to insult me again!

Vincent Van Gogh

It was always an interesting experience to talk with Mark. It was hard not to notice his rather wobbly stance and his asymmetrical features. His unruly light brown, curly hair, added to his rather odd appearance.

Mark always pulled at his ears; one while he spoke, the other while he listened. Because of this habit, Mark became known in our circle as Vincent Van Gogh. I even mistakenly called him Vincent once but corrected myself quickly. No harm done!

At one of our dances, Mark was faced with a dilemma. The hotel provided a vegetable platter at the back of the ballroom. Mark approached the table and put down the drink he had in his hand. He then proceeded to fill a plate with vegetables. He picked up his drink, at which point both of his hands were occupied. Just then, I went over to greet him. We began to talk. Poor Mark was bobbing his head left and right, trying desperately to figure out a way to pull at his ear. If only he had a third hand, but the only solution was to stop talking and walk away, which he did.

Mark asked me to go out with him at one point and I agreed. We planned to see a movie. Mark lived a couple of miles away from me. Having given Mark directions to my home, he was due to pick me up at 6 p.m. that evening. Six o'clock came and went. Then it was 6:15…6:30. I decided I had waited long enough. Mark was a no-show. My dad was home sitting on our porch. "Dad," I said, "Mark hasn't come and I'm not waiting any longer. I'm going out. If he shows up, tell him I left."

"O.K." dad replied.

As I got into my car and started driving down the street, I encountered Mark driving toward me. It was now 6:45 p.m. We both stopped. "Mark," I said, "What happened?"

"Oh, I couldn't read the street signs," he replied in an animated tone, as he bounced around the driver's seat.

I advise him, "You know, in college we wait 15 minutes for a full professor and then we leave. For you I waited 45 minutes and now I'm leaving. Besides, the movie already started. Why don't you go home. Let's forget about this date for tonight."

Mark was ecstatic! "What a wonderful idea," he cried. He began to throw kisses at me and told me I was "such a dear." It was as if a weight had been lifted from his shoulders. The jail door was open. Mark drove off and I went on to a program at my college.

Mark and I greeted each other at events in the future but we never attempted another date.

"She Lives At Home And Her Mother Doesn't Drive"

My girlfriends and I knew Kenny for several years. We would see him at the Westchester dances. Kenny was a thin, nervous fellow, whose light brown hair was combed like Fonzie's. None of us ever had any lengthy conversations with him but occasionally he would ask one of us to dance.

Kenny had a strange way of dancing; he would kick his legs up in the air. We always had to be careful on the dance floor to stay out of range of those flying feet, or we might get kicked in the shins.

Kenny had a crush on our friend Billie but she had no interest in him. One night, he began talking to me. After awhile, he confided that he really liked Billie but he would never ask her out on a date. "I couldn't ask her out," he said, "she lives at home and her mother doesn't drive!" I'm sure I looked puzzled at that remark but Kenny did not see the need to elaborate. I subsequently found out that Kenny also lived at home and his mother did not drive either. One of our friends suggested that Kenny must have felt that since both his and Billie's fathers were deceased, their mothers would be dependent on them. (O.K., I guess that made sense.)

About a month after Kenny told me that he could not date Billie, a bunch of us, including Kenny, were at a diner after a dance. Mary Jean kiddingly leaned over and loudly announced, "Hey, you know what? Billie's mother got her driver's license." Kenny just sat there without moving a muscle.

This is not the end of the Kenny story. A few months later, Kenny started dating Barbara. We called her "The Wax Museum" because the first time we saw her at a dance, she was sitting at a table with five other people and not one of them moved or spoke for what seemed like about 20 minutes. We were not sure if they were breathing. We were surprised to learn that Kenny had gotten together with Barbara. He was kind of shy and awkward; Barbara was quite the sexy dresser. She always wore tight-fitting outfits and looked as if she had been poured into them. We were afraid that if she sneezed her dress would blow apart. Well, the relationship blossomed and about six months later we heard that they had gotten engaged.

Then one night about a month after that, I was at one of our club's cocktail parties in Manhattan when Kenny showed up. He looked very disturbed as he walked over to me. I said hello and asked him how he was. He told me that Barbara had broken up with him. "What happened?" I asked.

He replied, "I don't know? She did say I never liked her mother's cooking." I did not think that was a very good reason to call off the engagement. Surely it could be remedied with the purchase of a cook book! Well, Kenny was completely baffled.

Several weeks later, Barbara came to a dance. As it happened, Billie and I were in the ladies room when

Barbara came in. She used to talk to us occasionally and I guess she felt the need to explain about Kenny. She said that she guessed we had heard that they had broken up. Then she told us the reason why she broke up with him. - He was a mama's boy! (So much for her mother's cooking!) Kenny and Barbara continued coming to the dances and trying to avoid each other. Then he stopped coming and so did she. Nobody knows what ever happened to either one of them.

Mama's Boys

Oh what a challenge competing with Mama! Don't try it – there is no contest. I found this out after attempting to maintain a relationship with, or relate to Mama's Boys.

First there was Julius. He desperately wanted to meet "a nice girl" and his mother did second the motion. She expressed her desire for him to be "settled" before she left this world. The problem? She was his world! Julius' father had died when Julius was 22; he was now approaching 40. Julius and I were introduced by a mutual friend. We seemed to have a lot in common and I looked forward to a new dating relationship.

Julius, a clean-cut fellow, had curly brown hair which he said that he permed. He sometimes spoke in a gruff manner in order to "put people in their place."

Julius asked me out after our first meeting at a neighborhood event. While we were out, he related his concern for his mother. It was evident that he felt guilty having left her for several hours, as he was shaky, nervous, and unable to concentrate on our conversation.

On our second date, Julius excused himself to use the phone to call Mama. While we ate dinner, he described an intricate code he and his mother had; one ring – he is at work, two rings – he is coming home, etc. He also described very detailed travel plans for himself and Mama. Car trips to various vacation spots, trips to different states to visit family members. They also scheduled their yearly physical exams together, including sitting side by side for blood drawing.

One time, I reminded Julius that his mother would not live forever and so he needed to consider making a life for himself without feeling guilty. He became extremely upset and cried, "Don't say that! Please don't talk that way!"

Julius cancelled or declined several dates with me because he had a previous engagement with his mother. On one occasion he actually chose to be with me over Mama and said to me, "I hope you're not upset because I didn't go with my mother."

Upon returning from their trips, Mama would fill me in on the particulars of their hotel room (yes, one room), and the spectacular terrace view, especially by the light of the moon.

In addition to spending all her time with Julius, Mama also belonged to a neighborhood senior center where she participated in many activities and outings, with Julius going along. He had a seat next to her on the tour bus.

After about six months of "dating," I had enough and read Julius the riot act. I informed him that he would have to stay with Mama until the end of her life. This came about after he suggested that I would have to "guarantee" to be her private duty nurse if we were married and she became infirm. I had a sick father, landlady, uncle and aunt at that time, so I considered that it might be prudent to open a nursing home where I would be the head nurse!

After our talk, Julius was very hurt and began to cry.

He did not want to break up but he could not pull away from his mother either. I spoke with him a few times after that during the following week but then I never heard from him again. The last I heard of him, he is still "married to the mom!"

Next came Reuben, whom I met at a dinner party. He had a lot to talk about and seemed interesting. Reuben had a squeaky little voice. At times, he sounded like he was whining. A nice guy, his dark hair and smooth features complemented his appearance.

Reuben asked for my phone number and wanted to take me out. He had mentioned his mother several times but I did not think it was significant. I figured he was just giving me a little background on his family.

Well Reuben called and had an excuse for needing to postpone our date; he had to take his mother to lunch. "O.K." I thought, "no big deal. We'll reschedule."

The following week Reuben called and cancelled another date. He had to take his mother to Atlantic City.

I did get to go out with him once, during which time he related the happenings of the outings he had had with Mama. I decided there was no room for me in this boat, so I did not push Reuben to meet on future occasions and he did not offer to plan anything for us.

I did not hear from him again. I am sure he is still enjoying Atlantic City but the only jackpot Reuben wants to win is Mama.

Skippy was attached to Mama on land and at sea. A

rather quiet, mysterious character, Skippy can always be spotted in a crowd. The sleeves on his shirts and jackets cover his hands past the tips of his fingers. He glides through the room with shoulders thrown back like a soldier, accentuating his pot belly. His receding dark hair, graying at the sides, is beginning to steal his baby face appearance.

Skippy would give detailed reports about life with mother whenever we saw him at a social event. Skippy has even brought his mother along with him to dances. He travels with her on a regular basis. They have seen most of these United States together. At one dance, they left early to finish packing for a trip the next day.

On one occasion, Skippy traveled on a cruise without his mother. He went with a group from our singles club. He called his mother three times from the ship in spite of the special telephone arrangements necessary at sea. I often wonder what Skippy would have done if he wanted to go home to Mama. Short of jumping overboard, he was stuck!

Skippy is often attracted to voluptuous women, better know as "bombshells". So far, Mama's apron strings are so long that Skippy cannot get close enough to another woman to do much of anything. But if those strings ever snap, it's Ship Ahoy for Skippy!

The Octopus

Rick was a new face in our club. He came to one of our events and seemed very friendly toward everyone. He related his experiences in trying to meet someone and said he was looking for "a nice old-fashioned girl."

Rick and I spoke for a while. It seemed that we held similar values and had some common interests. Although Rick had a rather sleek appearance, he presented himself as a very respectful, genuine fellow. At the end of the evening, Rick told me he would like to see me again. We exchanged phone numbers and I left feeling hopeful.

Rick called me during the week and we decided to go to a movie on Saturday night. When Saturday arrived, Rick came to my home to pick me up for our date. He was a real gentleman. He assisted me in putting on my coat; he held the car door as I got into his car. "Wow," I thought, "how nice this evening is going to be."

We arrived at Movie Time Cinema. As we entered, we chose two seats in the middle of the theatre, at the end of the row. The lights dimmed slowly as the movie feature began. I felt something on my right leg. "What's this?" I thought. "Oh, it's Rick's hand." As I looked up at him he was very attentive to the movie. His smooth features offering no expression. I shifted my leg and his hand fell away.

Five minutes later something was gliding across my back. "Now what?" I thought. "Oh, it's Rick's hand again." I looked over at Rick with surprise. He quickly withdrew his hand. "Good," I thought, "he got the message." Well, not quite. I spent the next two hours trying desperately to escape what had become an octopus.

At one point, after moving as far as I could to the end of my seat, I was slumped over and twisted into the shape of a pretzel – arms and legs intertwined and knotted all over. But to no avail. Rick continued to paw at me. Needless to say, the movie plot could not compare with what was going on in my seat. In addition to the fact that I could not watch it; I was preoccupied.

The movie ended and we exited the theatre. Upon returning to the car, Rick politely escorted me to the passenger side. I thought, "I'm going to get a reprieve now. He has to drive. Both hands will be on the steering wheel."

Rick had another idea. As we were riding home, he managed to steer the car with his left hand while his right hand was on my thigh. As we approached my block, I unhooked my seat belt. As the car rolled up in front of my home, I jumped out of my seat before Rick got a chance to touch anything else. This from a man who was looking for "a nice old-fashioned girl."

Pony Tail

We arrived at the Queens hotel, walked through the lobby and down the stairs to the ballroom where our dances were usually held. The doors were wide open but no one was there. We discovered that a function had been held there in the afternoon and that the room had not been cleaned for the evening. "Oh no!" we thought, "the dance is being held in the back dance room." Now there was nothing really wrong with the back room. It was smaller than our usual room, with the dance floor on the left side and the bar area on the right. The problem was that every time we had a dance in that room something unpleasant happened to Mary Jean or me. Well, what could we do? We headed for the back room and hoped everything would go well.

    When we entered, we saw that the lights were low and the room was crowded. Some friends called us over and we began to dance with them. When we got off the dance floor, a little guy moved in front of me. The top of his head reached a little above my waist. He had long black hair that was tied in a pony tail. He said to me, "You're an excellent dancer. Are you a dance instructor? Maybe you can give me lessons?" I smiled and said I was not and moved away from him since I detected insincerity in his eyes. I went over to some people I knew and stayed with them.

After awhile, my friends went off for various reasons and I was standing alone. Who walks over to me but "Pony Tail."

"I don't think you realized that I had wanted to talk with you," he said.

"Oh?" I feigned innocence.

He continued, "I must tell you that you are one of the most attractive women in this room!"

"Oh brother," I thought, "here it comes!" Then he asked me some questions about the dances: how many people usually attended, did they live in boroughs other than Queens? He told me his name but I really do not remember what it was. I was not paying much attention to what he was saying. I was trying to locate one of my friends to rescue me.

Just then, Mary Jean passed by. I introduced him to her hoping that she would be my deliverer. Pony Tail told her, right in front of me, "I can't believe how attractive you are!" (Wait a minute. That sounds familiar.) Mary Jean hurried on just as our friend Amy passed by. I introduced Pony Tail to Amy and he commented to her, "You are so attractive!" (Hey, get a new routine!) Gee whiz, I guess I must hang out with "the beautiful people." Amy continued on her way and I was left alone with him.

I was still trying to figure out how to get rid of him without being rude when it hit me. I knew exactly what to say. I waited for the right moment. Pony Tail was telling me that I looked like I was "with it." (O.K., you asked for it.) I responded, "Actually I'm very religious."

Pony Tail's eyes got as wide as two dinner plates and his tail twitched. "You're very religious?" he repeated.

I shook my head up and down vigorously and said, "Oh yes!"

Then he said, "what about your friend Mary? Is she religious too?" I nodded and said that she was. "And what about your other girlfriend?" (What was he doing, taking a survey?) Again I repeated the same thing. With that, Pony Tail said it was nice meeting me and hurried off. We never saw him again.

Nurse On Call

Warren often came into the clinic where I worked as a nurse. He accompanied his father, who was a regular patient.

Warren was a jolly character, not very tall, kind of pudgy, with deep brown inquisitive eyes. He owned a hair salon and offered discounts to the hospital employees. His unisex shop was always hopping, as it was located on a busy main street. He often asked me about my social life while he was styling my hair.

On one visit to the shop, Warren mentioned that he knew of a nice fellow he wanted me to meet. I cautiously agreed, having had my share of desperate blind dates.

Warren arranged for me to meet Xavier at a local diner. It was late afternoon on a weekday. I arrived early and went into the lobby of the diner to avoid the bright sunlight. I watched people walking by and eliminated the good looking men that came inside. I just was not optimistic.

Then I saw him. "It has to be him," I thought. Walking toward the diner was a rather obese older man with a double chin, dragging his right leg. His right eye was shut and he had a right facial droop. He also had receding dark hair and was drooling. My first impression as a nurse was that he must have had a stroke. The most striking thing about him was that he was carrying a perfect red rose.

When he got to the diner he approached me and we introduced ourselves. He handed me the rose as I tried to decide if this was a date or a private duty nursing assignment.

After being seated, we ordered a light snack. Xavier slurped a bowl of soup as I nibbled on a bran muffin. He then began to relate a sad account of his recent stroke. He described his appreciation for nurses and told me how the hospital nurses had slowly helped him to recover some of his faculties.

After about 45 minutes, we left the diner and Xavier walked me to my car. I adjusted my usual quick walking pace to his slow one. His weight also taxed him and he began to become short of breath. I almost felt like taking him to the hospital.

Upon reaching my car, Xavier said, "Are you going to tell your friends what a great guy you met today?"

I replied, "I'm going to tell them I met a most unique man." We said goodbye with no commitment to any future meeting.

I never spoke with Warren again, nor did I ever return to his shop. I never had any more contact with Xavier either.

It was just another blind date to add to the list, except this time I was a "nurse on call."

"You're Going To Pay Him Rent?"

The following tale is about our friend Karen, a sensible, cautious person who seemed to have lost her senses during a four month period several years ago.

Karen was a pretty girl, 5'3", with long brown hair, who resembled a young Marie Osmond. She had not been meeting any men, so she decided to try the personal ads. Her experience with that turned out to be a series of "dates from hell." Finally, she turned to a dating service in New York City. After several horrible encounters, Karen met Owen.

In comparison to the fellows she had been meeting, Owen seemed normal. He was six feet tall with blue eyes and short brown hair. Owen was seven years older than Karen, divorced with no children and had a blue collar job.

Karen and I used to meet at the subway station each morning and ride downtown together on our way to work; she got off at 59th Street while I rode one more stop to 42nd Street. During our rides, Karen would tell me about her dates with Owen. I noticed that their relationship seemed to be moving along rather quickly. Karen began to talk about an engagement after knowing him for only one month.

My friends and I met Owen when Karen brought him

to one of our club's dances. He did not talk much, perhaps because he did not know us, but he seemed like a nice fellow.

Then one Monday morning when I met Karen at the station, she was quiet and withdrawn, which was unusual for her. As we rode downtown, Karen told me that Owen had given her disturbing news when she had seen him the previous Saturday. He had told her that most of his adult life he had thought about becoming a priest and that he was seriously considering entering a seminary. I really did not know what to say to her except to say that I was surprised to hear this.

When I saw Karen the very next morning, she announced, as we were walking down the stairs toward the train, "We're getting engaged!"

I nearly fell down the steps! "What happened?" I gasped. Karen said that she had had a long talk with Owen over the phone the previous night and that they had decided on the engagement.

When I met Karen at the station the next morning, I was not prepared for the next installment of this saga. It was February, so we were dressed in winter clothes, including hats, scarves and gloves. Karen waved me over to her in a conspiratory manner. She slowly lowered the glove covering her left hand. To my surprise my eyes were dazzled from the glow of a sparkling engagement ring. "We got it last night," Karen revealed.

"How did you find a ring so fast?" I inquired.

"Oh", Karen said, "I've been looking at rings at this jewelry store for months and I've had my eye on this one."

The next morning (it's Thursday now), an excited Karen told me how she spent the day before running up and down the stairs in the building where she worked, showing her ring to people she knew in different departments of her company. Every morning for the next month, I received reports from Karen on the progress of her wedding plans. They were to be married in April. It would be at a justice of the peace with just the immediate family in attendance. They were planning to live in Queens where Owen resided.

As Karen gave me these updates, she related a number of things that made me uncomfortable. It sounded to me like Owen was becoming demanding and controlling. Owen told Karen that she owned enough clothes, so anything else she wanted to buy would have to be purchased at a thrift shop. He also did not like the brands of food she bought. On one occasion he took an inventory of the food in her refrigerator and then threw out most of the items. Owen felt that Karen should lose weight, therefore he was going to put her on a diet and weigh her on a regular basis.

Owen told Karen that the "Europeans" had the right idea when it came to working. He said that one spouse would take a year off from work while the other continued working. Then the following year, they would switch. Well guess who was going to take the first year off? Yes, Owen would stay home while Karen went to work.

Karen, being caught up in all of the excitement of the wedding plans, did not seem to be disturbed by Owen's behavior. Then one morning as we rode to work, Karen told me Owen's latest bright idea. He and his father were going to buy his brother's house in Queens and Karen would have to help out with the mortgage. I could not help blurting out, "You're going to pay him rent?" Karen had a confused look on her face. I said, "Karen, you're going to work, pay towards the mortgage, cook, clean, shop for food, get your clothes at a thrift shop and he is going to stay home?"

Karen responded with, "Well, I guess so?"

As it happened, the following Friday night, a number of our friends, including Karen and Owen, were going to a dinner dance sponsored by our club. At the dance, our friend Ben looked at Karen and asked her, "Are you happy?" She replied that she was but she later admitted that she had been getting chest pains every time she thought about the things Owen had been saying and doing. That weekend Karen broke up with Owen. Owen called her several times after the break-up but she never went back with him. During one conversation, he told her that he liked her friends so much that he wanted to keep in touch with us! We had been nice to him only because he was Karen's boyfriend. Luckily he did not ask her how to contact us.

Owen faded from the picture and for all we know, may have actually joined the seminary.

The Dishwasher

Andrew, a fellow I had met at a recent party, asked me out to dinner. A quiet guy with a rather droopy appearance, his thin frame and rounded shoulders resembled a plant that had not been watered for a while.

Andrew did not offer any input regarding our destination, so I chose a local diner which had a huge menu and great food.

After enjoying a few hours of good eating and nice talk, the check arrived. Andrew took out his wallet and opened it. Aghast, his sunken brown eyes popped out as he exclaimed, "It's empty!"

"Excuse me?" I said.

He repeated, "It's empty. My wallet is empty," his piercing voice attracting the attention of surrounding diners.

I looked over and responded, "Well, golly gee, it is empty. Well," I said, "I guess there's only one solution." I called over Andre, our waiter. "Andre," I said, "we have a dishwasher here; he's ready to start now due to the fact that he can't pay the bill."

"Wait!" cried Andrew, "this wallet has a secret compartment."

"You'd better not keep the secret too long," I said, "or you'll be going home with dishpan hands."

"Look," Andrew said, "there's fifty dollars in here." (Enough to pay the bill and then some.) What a relief. Disappointing for Andre though. He almost had himself another dishwasher.

"You Wanna Dance?"

And then there is Fred with the green complexion. He is one of those people who looked old since they were born. Fred is close to 50 years old but his thin gray hair and droopy demeanor make him look around 65. He always wears a fedora, which prompted our friend Jenny to say on more than one occasion, "Take off that hat! It makes you look like you're 100 years old!" Once when I was dancing with Fred, the song that was playing was "Staying Alive" by the Bee Gees. As I looked over at Fred, he seemed to be barely alive.

Fred is a nice guy but really thick-headed. Why is it that if a woman sees a male friend talking to a new woman at a dance, she would never go over and interrupt the conversation. Some men, on the other hand, march right over and barge right in! Fred is like that. How many times has he done that to me or one of my girlfriends? Usually I'll be talking to a new guy when Fred comes over, pulls at my sleeve and says, "You wanna dance?" I've tried to give him a look that says, "Not now, I'll dance with you later," but he never gets the message. When I tell him that I cannot dance with him because I'm talking with another guy, you know what Fred does? He joins in on our conversation! Once I was so frustrated that I walked away and left Fred talking with the guy. I do not think Fred realized that I was gone.

Well, the tables turned on Fred one evening at a dance. After talking with people and dancing for a while, Joan and I stepped outside of the dance room to get a breath of fresh air. A grinning Mary Jean brought over an uncharacteristically irate Fred. "Tell them what happened," Mary Jean prodded Fred. He was livid. "That guy always does this to me!" Fred barked. He then explained that he was talking with a new girl when a fellow he knew came over and joined their conversation. "I can't stand that!" Fred lamented. (As it turned out, that guy asked the girl to dance and she went off with him.) I looked right into Fred's eyes and said, "You know, there's a guy who does the same thing to us!" Fred was appalled. "That's so rude," he said. At that moment Joan was taking a sip of her soda. She nearly choked at Fred's remark.

Fred was upset for the rest of the evening. He kept shaking his head and grumbling. Usually after a dance, a bunch of us go to a diner for coffee. Well, Fred was too upset to join us. He just took the express bus home.

The "Help Me" Sign

Our friends Debbie and Ted are teachers of the deaf, so they know sign language. It was always interesting to watch them at a dance.

Usually at some point during the evening, Debbie would be dancing with someone at one end of the dance floor and Ted would be dancing at the other end. They would catch each other's eyes and start to sign across the room. They did not have to be concerned that the loud music would interfere with their conversation.

Whenever we asked them what they were signing about, they would admit that they were commenting to each other about the people they were dancing with. Of course no one watching would know what they were saying unless that person knew sign language. So, if they said anything uncomplimentary about their dance partners, it was likely that no one at the dance would be the wiser.

Debbie heard us girls complain that sometimes we got stuck with guys we really wanted to get away from. The reasons varied; some guys were sleazy, some nerdy and some scary. Debbie said she would teach us the "help me" sign so that we could use it to let our friends know that we needed assistance.

She instructed us to keep one hand outstretched with the palm up, then make a fist with the other hand, place the second hand into the palm of the first hand and then bring both hands toward your chest.

The sign worked pretty well. Whenever one of us was in a situation we wanted to get out of, we would look around for one of our friends, discreetly give the sign and our friend would come over and say something like, "I need your help. Could you come with me?" And so we would make our great escape!

Well, one night, our friend Annie was stuck with an obnoxious guy and was desperately looking around the room for one of us to help her. She kept doing the help sign but none of us was close enough to see it. A frustrated Annie kept signing until her hands were turning red but no one came to her rescue. Finally, she gave up, told the guy that she had to go to the ladies room and left him standing there.

For Whom The Bell Tolls

I was awakened early on a Saturday morning by the telephone. It was Oscar, a fellow I had met at a party the night before. He explained that he had asked the host for my phone number. He wanted to take me out that night to the movies where the rest of the party group was meeting. I agreed to go.

Oscar was a rather determined kind of guy. He had a stern appearance and an authoritative tone of voice. His square jaw and dark moustache were intimidating, as he rarely smiled. Oscar would blink excessively when he became irritated.

Oscar picked me up that night and we went out with the group. He asked me out on a few other dates after which he began to plan my lifestyle. He had an ideal in his mind for what was acceptable living.

First, he wanted to know why I had so many friends. He did not understand why so many people wanted to be around me. Oscar ordered, "When you come home from work, stay home. It's not necessary to go out, especially during the week." He also felt that we should be shopping in the same supermarket; in addition, we should be setting up joint shopping trips.

At that point, I decided to have less contact with Oscar, so he began to write me letters. He lived only several blocks away from me. In his letters he warned of the demise of our relationship if I did not see things his way. He advised me of the fact that I was lucky to have met him and I was selling myself short.

Finally in his last letter, sent express mail (from three blocks away), Oscar wrote, "Ask not for whom the bell tolls, the bell tolls for thee."

After that I never heard from him again. I was glad that the bell stopped ringing since it was a little cracked!

The Cardinal

Billie met Sam at a Westchester dance. We called him The Cardinal because his last name was the same as one of New York's famous cardinals. Sam was quite tall but looked somewhat anemic with long, stringy hair. He was very soft-spoken, which may have been one of the reasons why Billie enjoyed talking with him.

Sam lived in Putnam County and was not very happy when he learned that Billie lived in the Bronx. (She was G.U.) However, after dancing and talking with her for most of the evening, Sam asked Billie for her phone number, which she gave him.

Sam called Billie the next week and they arranged to meet halfway in Tarrytown that Saturday night. She would drive north and he would go south. Billie told us all about her date.

They met in the lobby of the Tarrytown Hilton hotel at around 6 o'clock. Sam suggested a restaurant in the area that he knew. They got into Sam's jeep and he drove them the short distance to the restaurant. As Billie ate her roast chicken dinner, she listened to Sam tell her about some addictive problems he had had in his life and his recovery from them. Sam had become a vegetarian and so he dined on a vegetable platter.

After dinner, they saw an action/adventure movie. Sam

brought Billie back to the Hilton for her to pick up her car. When they said goodbye, Sam said he would call her in a week.

Billie had a few more dates with Sam but each time, she would have to drive up to where he lived since he would never come down to the Bronx.

One Sunday, a few of us girls went to New York City for brunch. It was a German restaurant on the upper eastside. After an enjoyable meal, we stopped off at the ladies room before starting our journey back home. Billie was beginning to have some doubts about Sam. There was going to be a dance in Westchester that Friday and Billie was feeling uncomfortable about possibly running into Sam there, since he had not called her for several weeks. Billie said, "Do you think the cardinal will be there on Friday?"

A mature woman who happened to be in the ladies room at that time, assumed Billie was talking about the real Cardinal and said to her, "Well, at least you'll be in good company!"

Billie replied, "Oh, this is a different cardinal."

Another time we were at a Westchester restaurant for brunch (do you see a pattern here?) when, while waiting to be seated, Billie said, "I came here with the cardinal." She got the strangest looks from the people who were standing near us.

Well, when Billie started to protest about always having to drive to Westchester for their dates, Sam stopped calling Billie. He also stopped coming to the dances. He never did make it to the Bronx!

The Three Little Pigs
Here we relate three experiences in various stages of "pigdom."

Dirty Pig

A mutual friend suggested that Kendall and I meet. Brian said, "Mary Jean, this is a really nice guy. He has a good job, owns a house and has done well for himself. I was wondering if you would be interested in meeting him?"

My first thought was why is Brian campaigning for him? Then I decided, what have I got to lose? It could not be much worse than my past experiences, so I agreed.

Kendall called me and sounded nice enough. We spoke for almost an hour. He told me about his work, his house and stated he had been married but his wife had left him and he did not know why. (My ears went up at that point!) We arranged to meet the following week at a dance our club was sponsoring.

Friday night arrived and I went out wondering what, if anything would transpire. The night grew old and no Kendall. Needless to say, he stood me up! He was living up to my expectations: Expect nothing – Get nothing. Well, I thought, it may have been better than what I would have seen had he come – and how right I turned out to be about that!

I met Kendall several weeks later. Unbeknownst to me,

Brian had arranged for us to meet at a local community function. When Kendall approached me and introduced himself, my first thought was, "he looks like a dirty pig."

He looked like he had lived through a hurricane, with dirty clothes, including a dirty hat worn backwards. He began by apologizing for not showing up the night we were to meet. He said he could not call me because he had lost my phone number. (If I had a nickel for every guy who told me that...) As he extended his hand I noticed that it too was dirty. Then he related some rather serious health problems and being a nurse, I figured Brian got one thing right – he needed a nurse, (and a bath). I was polite and gracious, spoke with him for a few minutes and said goodbye. I thought, "He might own a house but obviously somebody came and took out the bath tub."

Quiet Pig

Dennis was a fixture at many of the social activities sponsored by one of the clubs I belong to. He was a veteran on the singles scene. However, he never spoke to me. As a matter of fact, I never observed him speaking much to anyone. He would stand there surveying the room, his jet black hair and mustache making him easily visible.

One night, I decided to wear something from my "bait collection." It was a very attractive green velvet dress, with a low square neckline and a slit on the bottom left side. I walked into the room and was greeted by none other than Dennis, displaying a mischievous expression on his face. At first, I was not sure that he was speaking to me. I had never heard his voice, so I looked at him. He spoke again,

"Hi, how are you?" So I returned the greeting and made history that night.

I concluded that it must have been the dress. My dress spoke for me and Dennis responded. In spite of the fact that I have subsequently worn items from the "ordinary collection," Dennis continues to speak to me. That was the night I got to know the quiet pig.

Sleazy Pig

After arriving at a dance one night, I began to walk around and greet some of the people there. I danced with a few friends and was on the way to get a drink when Arnold approached me. I did not know him well but had seen him at events in the past.

Arnold was a big guy with a solid physique. He stood tall as an oak tree and strutted through the crowd like a plow mowing down a field.

Arnold complimented me on my dress and began to talk about things he thought we had in common, his eyebrows rising above his square-rimmed eyeglasses. Suggesting that we converse for a while Arnold said, "Why don't you sit in my lap and we can talk about the first thing that pops up."

I promptly replied, "I really think we'll have very little to talk about," and continued on my way.

B.M.

Terry is very religious. She has made several trips out of the country to religious shrines. She is also somewhat aggressive and persistent. These are not especially good traits when guys are looking for "bubble-headed Barbie dolls." Male friends have actually admitted to me that the type of girl they want is beautiful, sexy, helpless and brainless. The ones they can control.

Terry has an annoying habit. She uses it when she wants to get away from a guy she is not interested in. After talking for a while to a guy at a dance, she will bring him over to one of us girls and introduce him. Then she will walk away and leave him with you. Now, that would not be bad if the guy looked like a movie star but this is never the case. He usually has the personality of a wet noodle. Of course then you have to figure out how to get away from him without being rude.

One evening, at a Long Island dance, I was talking with two attractive, intelligent guys. That in itself is a rare occurrence bordering on the miraculous. I had met one of them previously through one of my girlfriends. Terry spotted me and marched right over. She probably figured that since I had a "spare" I could give up one of them. I introduced her to the guys and we all chatted for a while with Terry monopolizing the conversation.

Terry informed us that she had recently moved from Queens all the way out to the eastern part of Long Island in Suffolk County. One of the guys asked her why she had moved so far away. Her response was, "The Blessed Mother brought me out there." With that, the guys' eyes sort of crossed and they remained stone-faced. No sooner had Terry made that remark when both guys said they had to go to the mens room. They took off, never to come near us again.

Movie Date

It was the dead of winter. The tempurature was about five degrees below zero, on a night a number of years ago. Damien had asked me out to the movies. He was a member of our neighborhood youth club at the time. We were all friends but many people paired off, dated and some eventually married.

Damien came to pick me up and received an initial greeting and licking from my beagle, Penny. Damien was visibly shaken after being approached by my timid dog. He was a "scary" kind of guy and socially backward. Damien was very tall and quite thin, with a tendency to become rather jumpy around people.

We left my house and traveled in his car to the movies. Not a long ride. It was a Saturday night and parking near the theatre was sparse but we found a space and walked to the box office.

Damien got in line and I stood aside. The moment of truth – he asked for ONE ticket, as I was shivering in the cold. He turned and looked at me. "What's wrong?" he said. "You don't have the money?"

I said, "I thought this was a date Damien!"

"Oh, I figured we're pals, was I supposed to pay?" he asked with a clueless expression on his face. At that point if I had not bought a ticket, I would have frozen to death, so I paid for a ticket and went in with him.

Obviously Damien had little or no dating experience. The pathetic look on his face told me we were "just friends."

Thom McCann

Our friends Annie and Kelly met at one of our dances a number of years ago and became close friends. They discovered that they lived less than 10 minutes from each other. They are about the same height, Annie is blonde and fair, while Kelly has both dark eyes and hair.

One evening, Annie drove to Kelly's, picked her up and then drove over to Ben's house. Ben is tall and slim with blue eyes covered by gold-framed glasses, unless he is wearing his contact lenses.

When Annie and Kelly arrived at Ben's, they got into his car and the three of them drove to my house to pick me up. Then we all headed for the Whitestone Bridge. Luckily there were no long lines at the toll plaza, so we got across the bridge without any major delays. We were off to the Uniondale, Long Island dance.

When we got there, we saw a number of our Queens/Long Island friends. "So how's the music tonight?" Ben asked.

"Who's the D.J.?" asked Kelly.

"Things are really hopping," one of our friends replied, as we walked inside towards the dance floor. Annie, Kelly and I took turns dancing with Ben, who is an excellent dancer.

During the evening we walked around, talked with some of our friends and caught up on the latest news. Annie and I had been dancing for a while and decided to take a break. We saw an empty table towards the back of the room, so we walked over and sat down.

Shortly thereafter, a short, dark-haired fellow came over and sat down at the table with us. The "portly one" told us his name and asked where we lived. As we were talking, Annie crossed her legs and dangled one of her feet. This fellow leaned over and began to brush Annie's shoe with his fingers. She and I both thought that he was brushing something off of her shoe but that was not the case. He then leaned over to me and said, "Women's shoes turn me on!"

I do not know what kind of expression I had on my face but Annie "got the message" and knew that something was wrong. "I need to take care of something," she announced as she jumped up out of her chair, "and I need you to help me," she said to me. We both took off.

We have seen this guy, who we nicknamed Thom McCann, at subsequent Long Island dances. At one dance, he had a camera around his neck and was taking pictures. The peculiar thing was that he was aiming the camera towards the floor. We finally determined that he must have been taking pictures of people's shoes. We never did see those pictures!

"I'll Have A Bagel"

I was on my way to do some chores on a sunny Saturday morning. I always had breakfast at home but this one morning I decided I would have coffee and a muffin at our local coffee shop.

I went in and was approaching the counter, when I heard my name, "Mary Jean, it's nice to see you." It was Gunther, a fellow I knew from our singles club. "Oh," he said, "I just finished eating but if you're getting in line, I think I'll have a bagel and sit and eat with you."

"What a break," I thought, just what I needed on an otherwise pleasant Saturday.

Gunther was a nerd. He was at least six feet tall but not in great physical shape. His potbelly and chubby face gave him an unbalanced appearance. His gray hair made him look older than his forty-something years.

Gunther was a lawyer and seemed to have done well professionally but was as social as a crocodile. "Well," I thought, "maybe he's planning to treat me to breakfast."

I ordered my muffin and coffee, his bagel and paid for everything. I went back with the tray, to the table where Gunther was ready to sink his teeth into more food. As I approached the table, Gunther looked like a dog waiting for a biscuit. I sat down and we began to eat. Gunther never thanked me for paying for his bagel and of course never offered to pay for my muffin and coffee.

Disco Bonnie and Sleazy Sal

Bonnie was a permanent fixture at the dances with her lean "Twiggy" figure and short dark hair. She must have owned only two dresses because whenever we saw her, she would be wearing either the pink one or the black and white one. Though different in style, the dresses had something in common, they both were well above her knees. The black and white had a slit up the back and each time she wore it, that slit got higher and higher.

Bonnie used to hold onto her pocketbook as if it contained the royal jewels. When she danced to a fast song, she would throw her pocketbook on the floor next to her and dance around it. When she danced to a slow song, that pocketbook would be pressed up against the guy's back. It's not as if she carried a lot of money with her. Only once did she come to the diner with us after a dance. She ordered a cup of tea but did not have enough money to pay for it, so one of the guys paid for her. We had heard that most of her salary went to pay for her high rent.

Bonnie never talked to women at the dances. She did not have the time to waste. On the rare occasion when she did talk to one of us, we knew it was a slow night.

It never failed that before the dance ended, Bonnie had given her number to a guy, had gotten his number, or both.

One night as she was leaving, I heard her tell a guy, "Call me by Wednesday. If I don't hear from you, I'm calling you!" Well, I guess those dates never worked out because the following week, Bonnie would be back at the dance and her routine would start all over.

Sal had a sleazy look. He was short and stocky with black hair. From his attitude we got the impression that he thought he was a real ladies man. One night when we arrived at a dance, Sal motioned to Mary Jean to come over to the table where he was seated. "I saved this table for you," he told her. He said that he liked her because she lived in the Bronx. "Bronx girls are with it!" he remarked. Then he told Mary Jean that she had "fire and passion in her eyes."

Mary Jean almost fell off her chair. She replied, "Well maybe you see compassion in my eyes. I am a nurse, you know."

Then it happened – Disco Bonnie got together with Sleazy Sal. They would meet at a dance and spend the evening together. They started dating and soon we did not see them anymore. We heard that they would constantly break up and then get back together again. This went on for several years.

Then one evening, Bonnie showed up at a Westchester dance. She came directly over to Mary Jean and me and asked how we were. She was very friendly and chatty. She told us that she was finished with Sal. "HE'S DIRT!" she exclaimed. "How could I have been so foolish?"

We saw Bonnie once after that night but Sal never returned.

Spike

One summer evening, a guy we called Jungle Jeff (because we often saw him wearing a safari outfit) brought a new girl to the dance. She had seen the dance advertised in a local paper and decided to call the phone number that was given. She spoke with the president of our club and told him that she wanted to come to the dance but needed a ride to get there. He asked her where she lived. He then suggested that she call Jeff, since she lived in Jeff's neighborhood. And that was how we became acquainted with Spike.

Spike, not her real name, had an unusual first name which sounded like something sharp. One night, after she had been to a couple of our dances, Mary Jean made an honest mistake and said, "Oh look, there's Spike!" The name was actually quite appropriate because she looked like a roller derby queen, Big, Bad and Bold! Spike had short, platinum-colored hair, was about 5'10", weighing in at around 200 pounds. Jeff was about the same height as Spike but had a slight build.

Another one of our friends also made a mistake with her name and referred to her as "Nails" one night. Of course, Spike never knew the nickname we called her, or we would have been in big trouble.

Jeff used to give Disco Bonnie a ride to the dances since she did not drive and lived only a few blocks from him. However, once Spike and Jeff started dating, Spike told Jeff in no uncertain terms that he was to stop giving Bonnie any rides.

Once we were at a house party when Jeff and Spike arrived. Jeff, being very friendly, started talking with Mary Jean whom he had known for a number of years. Well, Spike was not pleased. She ordered in a loud voice, "Jeff, get over here!" Jeff went scurrying over to her. Mary Jean was stunned and a little scared. From then on, neither Mary Jean nor I ever spoke to Jeff again for fear of being attacked by Spike.

Spike and Jeff got married and as far as we know are still together, she giving orders and he obeying them.

Tod, Tad, Toad

Tod was friends with our friend Molly and hung out with her crowd at our dances. He was a tall, quiet guy who liked to dance. He usually wore casual clothing to the dances.

I often talked and danced with Tod. On one occasion, he told me that he had recently broken up with his girlfriend and was trying to get back into the social scene. Since it was springtime, my friends were planning a number of outdoor group activities such as going to the Bronx Zoo and the Westchester County Fair, so I invited Tod to join us. Each time that the day came for the trip, Tod would call with some reason why he could not make it. (His sister was coming over; his refrigerator was broken and he was waiting for the repairman.)

Meanwhile, Mary Jean and I began to notice that there were times when Tod was very talkative and friendly. At other times, he was very playful. Still others, all he would do was complain about his health problems. It was as if he were different people. We soon learned that quite a few of the girls at the dances believed that Tod had multiple personalities.

This led us to give each personality a different name: Tod was quiet; Tad was friendly; Toad was nasty; Ted had the health problems; Tyler was "kissy." When we saw him at a dance, we would identify who he was that night. If Mary Jean talked with him first, I would ask her, "So who is he tonight?"

Her response would be something like, "Oh, it's Ted. He was telling me all about his latest ailments," (and getting a free nursing consult as a bonus.)

There were times when he would change personalities while you were talking with him. You would be talking with, say for instance Tad, when all of a sudden Toad would make an appearance and say something very rude. That was the signal to make an excuse and get away from him.

One evening, I must have been talking with Tad because he had been very nice and I told him that he was "a prince."

Mary Jean commented, "A toad that turned into a prince." Of course he did not understand the significance of her statement.

Tod is still around. His usual pattern is that he meets a girl and they start dating, so we do not see him for a few months. Then, when the relationship starts to turn serious and he has to make a commitment, Tod breaks it off and returns to the dances. Sometimes the girl breaks up with him. Once, he was dating a girl for about six months. We assumed that she had not met Toad (the nasty one) yet but once she did, that would be the end of the relationship and Tod, Tad, Toad would be back at the dances.

"Show Me The Dollar!"

Buck was very popular with the ladies. He was handsome, athletic and could be quite charming but he had a dark side. He was moody and at times his behavior was bizarre. Buck was divorced and although he did not go into details, apparently whatever had happened with his ex-wife had soured him towards other women.

Buck said that his "best girl" was his dog Queenie, a rottweiler. He even brought Queenie to one of our dances. No, he did not bring her inside, he left her in his car. After the dance we all went to a diner. In the parking lot of the diner, Buck made Queenie do some tricks for us. He put a hamburger and bun on her nose and she flipped it up and caught it in her mouth.

Buck often told us stories of his dating experiences. One time he had gone to a club in Queens and met an attractive girl named Melanie. They were talking for a few minutes when Melanie gave Buck her business card and asked him to call her. She then left him and went over to the bar.

As the evening progressed, Buck observed a pattern in Melanie's behavior. She would talk to a guy for about five minutes, hand him her card and move on to someone else. Buck mentioned Melanie's behavior to his friend Karl.

"Oh her," Karl said, "she does that all the time. She gives her number to lots of guys and then she evaluates them when they call her on the phone. If she thinks there is potential, she goes on a date with the guy."

At the end of that evening, Buck noticed Melanie talking with a guy as she was looking for another of her business cards. Unfortunately, she had run out of cards. Buck went over to them, handed the guy the card she had given him and said, "Here, you can have mine; I won't be needing it."

At the dances, some of us girls had complained to Buck that we often were stuck with guys we wanted to get away from. Buck had the solution – he said all we had to do was catch his eye, wave a dollar bill (which he would later take) and he would come over and rescue us. I never took him up on that offer however, one night the tables turned when Buck was cornered by Serena.

Serena had black hair when we first met her but she never stuck with one color. Over the course of several months she was a platinum blonde and a flaming redhead. Serena was slightly overweight and about 5'6" to Buck's 5'10".

Buck had gone out with Serena once but really was not interested. Serena, however, became obsessed with him. She called him constantly, left messages on his phone machine, and parked outside his apartment for hours.

The night that Buck was cornered by Serena, he looked desperately around the room as he tried to figure out what to do. I caught his eye as I took a dollar bill out of my pocketbook and waved it at him. He understood I was telling him that I would rescue him for a dollar. I was kidding about the dollar. Buck looked so pathetic as I walked over to him and Serena.

I said that a friend of his was looking for him and for him to follow me. Buck was very grateful that I got him away from Serena. Eventually she stopped harassing him and dropped out of sight.

Gentleman John

We were at a Westchester dance one Saturday evening, when John approached Billie and asked her to dance. John was an average looking fellow, slightly overweight but pleasant. He worked for the county. Billie spent part of the evening with him even though she was not attracted to him.

John asked for her phone number several times but she kept making excuses to avoid giving it to him. Several of her friends who saw her with John, told her that she should give John a chance. "You keep saying that you want to meet a nice guy and when you do, you don't want to go out with him," Tommy said. Billie was undecided.

When the dance ended, about 15 of us, including John, went across the street to the diner. Billie was still unsure but her friends encouraged her to go out with John. At the diner, the waiters placed several tables together to accommodate the group and then left us the menus. Billie did not want to sit next to John but he managed to take the seat next to her. Some people ordered breakfast (eggs, pancakes), some got hamburger platters, while others ordered muffins or bagels.

When the bill came, John grabbed it and said, "I'll take care of this!" We were all shocked. Some of us protested but John was adamant. Tommy told Billie, "He's trying to impress you." When we were about to leave, Billie finally relented and gave John her number. We said goodbye to our friends and drove back to the Bronx. It was about 2 a.m. by the time we got home.

At 7 a.m., Billie's phone rang. It was John. "I just left you!" Billie exclaimed. "Well I wanted to ask you out for Friday night," John replied. He said he would pick her up for dinner and a movie, so Billie gave him the directions to her house. (Obviously she was not G.U.)

Billie was not very excited about this date but she decided to take her friends' advice and give him a chance. When she got home from work on Friday, Billie showered, washed her hair, put on a nice suit and waited for John.

When the doorbell rang, Billie opened the door and was surprised to see John in sweat pants, a stained t-shirt and sneakers. The next shock came when they went to his car. As Billie went to sit on the passenger side, she had to move empty fast food containers and garbage bags to make room for herself. The car windows were dirty. Billie could not figure out how John could see out the front window to drive. Billie started to wonder if she had made a mistake by agreeing to go out with him.

Billie told John how to get to a nice Italian restaurant in her neighborhood. She was a little embarrassed being dressed up while John looked like he was going jogging.

As they ate dinner, Billie noticed that John had a peculiar habit. John had tucked his napkin into the waistband of his pants. He would take a bite of food, remove the napkin, wipe his mouth and then tuck the napkin back into his waistband. After awhile, this ritual was driving Billie crazy. She watched his protruding stomach go up and down as he removed and replaced the napkin. Billie was thinking, "And I gave up an evening of laughing with my girlfriends for this?" Finally dinner was over and they left for the movie.

Billie directed John to a local movie theater. When they sat down in the theater, Billie took the end seat on the aisle as John sat next to her. During the movie, John kept getting closer and closer to her as Billie leaned further and further into the aisle. "When will this evening be over?" she lamented.

The movie ended and John drove Billie home. He asked her what she was doing the following weekend. She said she was going dancing with her girlfriends. John offered to drive all the girls to the dance in his car but Billie said it was not necessary. Then John asked if he could follow the girls to the dance in his car. Billie vetoed that idea too. The car stopped in front of Billie's house, and John leaned over to kiss her goodnight. Billie closed her eyes and pictured Ricky Martin.

As she closed the car door, John told her he would call. John did call several times but Billie kept giving him excuses why she could not go out with him. He finally got the message and stopped calling.

They Just Don't Get It

Some girls can be really cruel when they turn down a guy who asks them to dance. They can give him a look that says, "Why would I want to dance with you?" I heard one girl say, "Get away from me. I didn't come here to meet you!" On the other hand, my girlfriends and I try to be nice to guys even when we are not interested but they misinterpret our kindness and we are stuck with them for the evening.

Once, I was dancing to a fast song with a new guy, when Barry, a nerdy-type fellow, complete with ball point pens in his shirt pocket, whom I had always been polite to, came onto the dance floor and surprised us by joining us. The guy I was dancing with did not know what to do, so he gave up and walked off leaving me with Barry. The song ended and I started to walk away when Barry said, "I have to go to the men's room but I'll be right back."

I just nodded my head while thinking to myself, "Who cares?" For the rest of the night, I was in perpetual motion moving around the room to avoid Barry.

Then there is Ron, a nice guy but one who sort of blends into the room. He is a fellow who has S.A.D. (Socially Arrested Development). Ron is approaching 40 but socially he acts like a teenager. At the dances, Mary Jean spends some time talking and dancing with him but she also does those things with other men there. Ron thinks he and Mary Jean are on a date.

At the dances, Ron usually gets there early and waits for Mary Jean outside the ballroom, or in the lobby. Then when she arrives, he goes inside with her. Of course he never pays for her but only for himself. One cold winter evening I arrived at a dance and saw Ron pacing back and forth in the parking lot. He was not wearing a coat.

"Is Mary Jean coming tonight?" he asked when he saw me.

"Yes, she'll be here," I answered. When I got inside, I saw that Mary Jean was already there.

"I got here early," she said. I told her that Ron was waiting outside for her without a coat on. "Oh no," she replied, "I better go out and get him before he catches pneumonia."

Last but not least there is Alex, whom we have known for a number of years. You can only take so much of him before he starts to get on your nerves. Alex used to wear a Morris the Cat t-shirt at our club picnics. He actually resembles a cat with his round face and his moustache that looks like whiskers.

One evening, Alex said to Mary Jean, "We've both been searching for a partner when maybe what we need is each other?"

Mary Jean replied, "Alex, why ruin a beautiful friendship by having a relationship?"

Short Takes

The Chiropractor
Andy asked me to dance to a slow tune. He had his arms around me as I began to feel digging in the vertebra of my back. "Andy," I asked, "are you a chiropractor?"

"Excuse me?" he said.

"Well," I said, "I really feel like I'm getting an adjustment." Andy did not seem to comprehend the scenario and I never found out what kind of work he really did.

The Coupon Man
Eric and I met at a party. He seemed like a very considerate and sincere person. He told me about the recent loss of his father. "Oh," I said, "I'm sorry to hear that."

He replied, "Funerals are so expensive these days. I had to shop around. I bargained with a few funeral homes before I got a good reasonable package. My mother was appalled. She just didn't understand."

Then, as the evening drew to a close, Eric asked me out. He said he had a very nice restaurant in mind but there was to be a delay. He said he wanted to wait until he could find a 2 for 1 coupon. Buy one dinner, get one free. I never heard from Eric again. I guess he is still looking for that coupon.

Where's The Beef?
I was at a fund raiser dinner-dance when I spotted a nice looking, neatly dressed fellow at the next table. "Gee," I thought, "I should go over and say hello." I approached him and introduced myself. "Hello, I'm Mary Jean. How are you tonight?"

He replied, "My beef is dry." I was hoping he was referring to the prime rib dinner we had just enjoyed.

"Pardon me?" I said.

"My beef is dry," he repeated, "it needs gravy." I realized as soon as he opened his mouth that he was not the interesting man I thought he was – and he never did get his gravy!

"Take Off That Head Band"
Our shy, refined friend Laurie was sitting at a table at a Manhattan dance one evening, when a fellow sat down beside her. After a few minutes of small talk he said, "You really don't have a sexual look about you. Take off that head band and let your hair fall down. You need to wear shorter skirts and plunging necklines!"

Poor Laurie was aghast. She replied, "I think it's time for a drink." With that, she got up and left him sitting there.

The Personal Ad
Gabrielle, a nurse who worked with Mary Jean, decided to place a personal ad in a local newspaper. Among the things she said was that she was "5'3" and into meditation."

When she got the paper, she looked through it and discovered that the Ad said she was "6'3" and into medication."

A fellow saw her ad and called her. She said he sounded like he was high on something. Apparently he thought they had something in common. "Well," Gabrielle admitted, "I'm a nurse, so I am into medication!"

The Pointless Sisters

You have heard of the Pointer Sisters? Now you are going to hear about us sisters who are pointless! How did we get our name? Well, one Christmas night several years ago, a group of us girlfriends were visiting Billie and her sister Betty. We were discussing the futile attempts we had made to try to meet and/or date men. We decided to confer upon ourselves PhD degrees, (Pointless, Hopeless and Depressed). We all had done our dissertations at various dances and other desperate singles events. That night, we decided to announce our identity to the world on t-shirts.

The next day, December 26th, we went to a local store to purchase our t-shirts. Each of us chose a color, red, yellow, blue, pink and turquoise with "Pointless Sisters" written in black across the shirt in block letters. Very elegant! Now it was official – we were truly pointless.

Periodically, Billie would mention that we all should go out to Coney Island some weekend. She said that she did not mind driving out to Brooklyn since she worked nearby and was familiar with the area. Finally one September Saturday, we made plans to go. Billie suggested that we wear our Pointless Sisters t-shirts. We thought that would be fun, so we did.

We met at Billie's house (we all lived in the Bronx then)

and we piled into Billie's car. There were four of us "sisters."

Billie checked the gas gauge and realized that she needed gas for the trip, so she drove over to her local gas station. It was a warm, sunny day, therefore we were not wearing any jackets or sweaters over our t-shirts.

Billie pulled into the gas station and told the teenage boy to, "Fill it up."

As he set up the pump, he looked into the car. "What does that say on your t-shirts?" he asked.

Billie said, "Oh we're the Pointless Sisters. We're a singing group. We're going to Coney Island right now for a singing job."

The boy's eyes widened and his eyebrows lifted. He finished, Billie paid him and we were off.

We arrived at Coney Island about 50 minutes later. It was not easy finding a parking spot but after driving around for about 10 minutes, Billie squeezed her car into one. By then it was around noon, so the first thing we did was to head for a Nathan's hot dog stand. Those hot dogs, french fries and sodas were really great!

Billie, the dare-devil of our group, was anxious to ride the roller coaster. Fran, who is equally courageous, went with Billie to get on line for the "Cyclone," while the rest of us chickens waited on terra firma.

The afternoon turned into early evening as we walked along the boardwalk, went on some rides and played some games.

While we were walking across the sand, a fellow standing in front of an exhibit was talking into a microphone. We were not paying much attention to what he was saying as he directed the crowd in front of him to "come in and see the live sharks." As we walked towards him he must have gotten a good look at our t-shirts because all of a sudden he announced, "Ladies and Gentlemen, it's the POINTLESS SISTERS." It took several seconds to realize that he was referring to us. The crowd in front of him eagerly turned around to look for the "celebrities." That fellow really got into it saying into the microphone, "So girls, how's the album doing? Is it selling? Do you have a gig up on the boardwalk?" We nodded in agreement and kept on walking.

There is a follow up to this Coney Island story. About a month later, on a Saturday evening, we were driving out to a Long Island dance. It happened to be Billie's turn to drive. The same group of us were in her car as she pulled into the same gas station; however, this time we were dressed for the dance and we had coats on over our dresses. The same teenage boy was pumping gas. He looked at the car, looked at us and exclaimed, "I know you. You're famous!"

Several years later, three of us "sisters" took a trip to the Canadian Rockies. We decide to take our t-shirts with us. After all, this was an opportunity to introduce the "Pointless Sisters" outside of the USA.

During our trip, we perused our itinerary, trying to decide what the best day and activity would be for us to go "pointless." It came during our tour of the Banff Springs Hotel, which looked like a museum housed inside of a palace. We were wearing our "pointless" t-shirts when we went downstairs to the tour bus. There were a number of different reactions from the other members of our tour. Some people seemed puzzled by our shirts, some just laughed, while others asked what it meant, so we filled them in on our "pointless history." At the Banff Springs Hotel, two strangers approached us and asked if they could take our picture. We were in a stately looking room, decorated with historical items and furniture. We three "sisters" sat down on a royal looking sofa, covered in red velvet, adorned by gold trim. It was there that we had our picture taken for posterity.

A few days later, we wore our t-shirts again on the tour bus as we traveled across the country. We had finally made it – The Pointless Sisters were international!

Epilogue

Well, now we wrote the book. Can you see why we were compelled to put these stories down in print? Truth is stranger than fiction. What feelings did these stories arouse in you? Shock, amusement, disbelief, laughter, disgust? We have experienced all of the above! In spite of our experiences, we still have not lost our sense of humor.

We hope you have enjoyed this book. You can be sure that whatever has happened to you has probably happened to someone else. However, there is always a story that tops all the rest.

For those of you who are single, good luck in your singles pursuits. No matter how discouraging the situation appears to be, always look for the comical side.

As we are still part of the singles scene, there will always be an opportunity for another story, as we continue to meet, "Pigs, Nerds and Macho Men."